A Grieving Mother

Marion M. Jones

authorHOUSE®

AuthorHouse™
1663 Liberty Drive
Bloomington, IN 47403
www.authorhouse.com
Phone: 1 (800) 839-8640

Published by AuthorHouse 09/22/2017

ISBN: 978-1-5462-0863-1 (sc)
ISBN: 978-1-5462-0862-4 (e)

Table of Contents

Chapter One.. 1
The Event Leading Up To His Death

Chapter Two.. 8
Pre-Planning Activities And Thoughts

Chapter Three 9
Funeral Arrangements: When & How Were They Made?

Chapter Four 11
The Impact Of Death Was So Painful

Chapter Five..16
How Did This Grieving Pain Impact Work?

Chapter Six... 19
My Years Of Grief 1St Thru 6Th

Chapter Seven.. 50
How Are You Feeling Now?

Chapter Eight 52
What Has Been Most Helpful Along Your Grief Journey?

Chapter Nine... 58
Who Has Been Helpful To You?

Chapter Ten.. 60
Impact Of The Death On Other Family Members
     Subtitles:
       * The organizations that were helpful to me.
       * What has been least helpful?

Chapter Eleven.. 64
What Has Pushed Your Buttons (Irked You To No End?)

Chapter Twelve 67
Things That Was Helpful Going Through My Grief
    Subtitle:
    What else have you done in the following areas?

Chapter Thirteen.. 71
My Messages And Suggestions To The
Bereaved & Newly Bereaved.
    Subtitles:
    * What lesson have you learned?
    * What do you wish you had done differently?

Helpful Scripture 75

The End Comments...76
About The Author 79

The Short Story of a Grieving Mother

In Loving Memory of my son TJ & Coping with Grief

by Marion M. Jones

Dear Readers,

This is a true story about my grief journey of the death of my son TJ, which I started writing over 12 years ago. I hope everyone that reads my story walks away with healing, recovery, and a spiritual uplifting. You see, even in death, you can come alive again,.... think about it.

Though we may die, Jesus says, "I am the resurrection and the life. He who believes in me, though he may die, he shall live." (John 11:25). Thank you in advance for considering reading my story, in the name of Jesus!

Who was TJ? A SYNOPSIS OF HIM:

He was born in Washington, DC on January 2, 1980, he grew into a fine young man, but at the tender age of 22, the tragic death of my son TJ definitely had a profound impact on me and my family and anyone who knew him. He will impact our lives forever. My son was a lovable guy, always smiling and very charming. He will be in our hearts forever.

Now, how do I begin to tell you how the death of my son TJ, my youngest, and my best friend has impacted my life? This will be the most difficult thing I have ever had to do in life, but through my faith, I'm moving forward.

Testimonials

What others are saying about this book:

- I am the proud daughter of this amazing new author Marion M. Jones! I'm so excited for everyone to read my mom's book called "A Grieving Mother". As a reader, and not just her daughter, I was moved by my mother's heart-felt stories. Every one of them touched me and allowed me to see things from her perspective, which was wonderful and gratifying. This book was definitely a tear jerker for me, but in a therapeutic healthy way. Just when I thought I was over grief, this book made me realize I wasn't. I needed more healing and it helps me grieve in a more positive way. I'm so thankful for my mom for sharing her story. This woman will show you how brave and courageous she is. I thank

God for her everyday and feel blessed for her to be my mom. –TaSha Douglas

- "All parents of loss children should be thanking you for writing this book" – Friend Patricia Robinson of Maryland

- If you want to understand pain and grief, please read "A Grieving Mother" – Aunt Irene

Special Thanks

Special Thanks; some authors like to praise their family for supporting them during the book-writing journey. This right-hand page was used historically by writers to acknowledge their patrons: the persons or institutions that supported them financially while they wrote.

Dedication

This is a special thanks to all the Parent(s) of loss love ones in recognition of their pain and grief. Also, special dedications to family, friends and support groups that helped me on my journey that lead me through my purpose and plan that God has for me.

To my husband, Eric, who has always been there through my good and bad times. To my daughter TaSha, my sons (twin) Eric & Derrick, my grand's: Jasmine, Jaila and Lydell of whom I love very much. I also dedicate this to my many other families members, friends, and church family who has supported me throughout my grief process.

Recognition of others:

- Mary L. Young (Mom)
- Edward & Jessie Jones (In Laws)
- Aunts: Bretina Dreher, Irene Young, Tia Shepherd, Dee Anderson and Faith Lyles
- Kenny Lyles (Brother – who always believe in me)
- Patricia Robinson
- Cynthia White
- Rene` Michelle Fenwick (Cuz)
- Edward Holton Jr. (Cuzzo) – Front & Back Cover Designer of my book (g3mini-graphix.com)
- Theresa Brown Phillips
- Malores Hall
- Roni Stubbs
- Anetra Tucker
- Tracey Jones
- Tracy Felton
- Craig & Jarris Jones
- Glenda Lomack
- Olivia Gunter (R.I.P)
- Alicia Mann
- Tomioka Hughes
- Jennifer Perez

- Cassaundra Reed
- Pat Butler
- Yvonne Brown
- Belinda Clark & Family
- Melissa Lyles & Family
- The Holly Family

Epigraph

If A Husband Dies, The Wife Is Called A Widow.

If the wife dies then her husband is called a 'widower.

If A Child's Parents Die, The Child Is Called An Orphan.

Why Isn't There A Word For A Parent That Loses A Child?

Introduction

This book represents the true story of how a grieving mother processes her grief. The process of grief is a message in my life that is the purpose and plan of God; His will, not my will, must be done.

You don't have to face grief alone; the spirit of God within you, will give you strength, courage, and..... your life back, through Jesus Christ. As you read each inspirational message, know that some of the words written were from families and friends to encourage me. In addition, you will see some pictures and Bible verses to speak to your heart and uplift your spirit. I believe as you read the gravity of the story, it will allow you to be in the presence of the Lord through your grief journey.

Our children have died at all ages, and for many different causes, and each one of our stories is very unique. Also unique is our grief journey as we all move forward through our lives. It is important that we all tell our stories of how we coped having experienced the death of our children and loved ones.

This is a very meaningful memorial to my sons, and sometimes a very painful place. Nevertheless, I can tell as of today, I'm *moving forward* and in less pain, as the years go by. Sometimes, nonetheless, pain makes you ask the right questions, so keep that in mind as you read this short story of a grieving mother.

Let's begin the journey...

I'm introducing this book also, as a "Self-Help Book" to guide you to release some of your pain. My prayer is that it becomes an invaluable resource to those that have experienced the loss of a friend or loved one and may be grieving. It is intended to help guide them through the painful process of grieving. It will inspire and encourage you to move forward one-day-at-a-time. It's also my hope, prayer that it gives you comforter and inspiration for you and others.

My son was affected by seizures which could easily have taken his life. Seizures are caused by abnormal electrical discharges in the brain. Symptoms may vary depending on the part of the brain that is involved, but seizures often cause unusual sensations, uncontrollable muscle spasms, and loss of consciousness.

Some seizures may be the result of a medical issue and problem. Low blood sugar, infection, a head injury, accidental poisoning, or drug overdose can cause a seizure.

A seizure may also be due to a brain tumor or other health problem affecting the brain. In addition, anything that results in a sudden lack of oxygen to the brain can cause a seizure. In some cases, the cause of the seizure is never discovered, which is what happen in my son TJ's case.

When seizures recur, it may indicate the chronic condition known as epilepsy. This is what he had, and yes, it can be fatal. A person with epilepsy can die as a result of illness, injury due to his condition, or suddenly, for no apparent reason. Again, although TJ could have died due to seizures, he didn't, instead, someone murdered him with a gun (Tech-9 as they called it in the report), shot 9 times to the torso and upper extremity perforating lungs and heart.

Reading the report, sicken me, inside and out, knowing someone could do such a horrible thing to my son. Nevertheless, I live with it every day, even as I move forward. The real life of having to move forward is still just so painful.

As you read this story, imagine having to go through something like this happening to a loved one. This is something not even wished on the worst of enemies and I had to face such a tragedy. I was at my job at NASA Goddard, Maryland when I found out by way of my mother and husband who were calling about the same time. I would go to the crime scene as well as hear it on the late night news (Fox, Channel 5).

Brace yourself and join me on this journey as you will now hear my story, the pain I endured, grief incurred, and my arrival to deliverance and recovery.

Welcome to my story!!

Let's continue this journey together!

To begin, let me know, what's your pain?
Book Reader:

_____

_____

_____

_____

_____

_____

May the grace of God, be with whomever reads this short story book project, in loving memory of my sons Thomas Bertrum Holly, III also known as T.J., and later on before the end of my story, my oldest son James' life, which ended in an untimely death.

If you've lost someone, list their names:

Book Reader:

_____

_____

_____

_____

_____

_____

_____

_____

_____

_____

_____

_____

_____

_____

Chapter One

THE EVENT LEADING UP TO HIS DEATH

"The Story of a Grieving Mother"

I remember receiving an early morning call from T.J., just after midnight on July 9, 2002. He called me from my mother's home in Fredericksburg, Virginia, to ask for prayer. I read some scriptures and was to meet him for his doctor's appointment due to the seizures/epilepsy he was having.

He asked for prayer again, he told me that he was very happy about his life, he told me, "I'm a good mother and he was glad I had married Big Eric". He said that sometime people in life want you gone, because they don't understand the changes in your life as a person or even a human being; they just don't like you.

I knew what he meant, because in my life time people didn't even know me, but dislike me for no reason (TJ said, "Mom, people just hate on you or dislike you because you do good, they want you gone, but if God loves you, that's all that matters"), so I told TJ "we live in a world full of hate, envy, resentment and jealousy, but we have to focus on God and his plans". It was late but, me and TJ always talked at late hours; I told him I love him and he said "I love you Mom always". I didn't know at the time these would be the last words I would ever hear from my son mouth.

July 9, 2002 seemed like an ordinary day. It was a beautiful day as I went to work, but I continued to think about my son TJ; he weighed heavy on my mind. I would pray that morning as I normally did, and though I was at peace, there was still something I couldn't figure out, as I was still bothered at the same time.

I called my daughter TaSha and we went to lunch on that clear sunny day. I was happy and sad at the same time. *Has that happen to you ever?* Although I prayed and sang, I still had the uneasy feeling. Again, it was a beautiful sunny day that didn't seem as though it would ever end and TaSha said "mom we will be okay – God will get us through".

My story, our journey….

It was July 9, 2002, a very warm day. I went to work that day although I suppose to be at home. I was to meet my son TJ at his doctor's appointment that evening, but suddenly my daughter TaSha and I had decided to go to lunch but I could feel something was wrong. We both worked for NASA and we were in my daughter's office after lunch

As my daughter went to the restroom, I started dialing

my son's cellphone number and a recording came on saying "The person you are trying to reach is no longer available", I kept dialing, thinking I must have dial the wrong number, but it kept on repeating and same message over and over again "The person you are trying to reach is no longer available." By this time I went to pick up the office phone to dial again and my husband was on the other end. He said, "honey don't go anywhere I'm coming to pick you up" and I asked "for what, I'm trying to call TJ" (at that time I had tears in my eyes), but my husband said again, "honey don't go anywhere."

I hung up the phone and called my mother in Virginia, my mom said, "Marion where are you" and I said "I'm at work in TaSha's office, mom where is TJ? I thought he had a seizure due to the fact he had been having them since, August 13, 1998 and I knew he could die from it, that's why I thought maybe he had a seizer and died.

My mom says no Marion, but......(this was one of my worst fears). My mom asked "Marion where is your boss", I said "tell me" and she said "he is dead", I didn't want to believe it and I screamed, everyone came running, my daughter came running from the bathroom, the scream was so loud and I went in the next office and told her and she screamed. I still didn't know he had been shot until I got to the crime scene, and saw the yellow tape rope around the car with TJ.... shot up.

This was something like in the movies, I just said "I'll wake up in a moment,...but he never came back home, and now that I'm writing this. I now know that he will not be coming home, at least not in this life time.

As I was near, then at the crime scene, I saw one of my son's legs hanging out the driver's side of the door and I cried and cried. I looked around and people where everywhere, then I saw this woman in white, walking through the crowd, but it seemed as no one was seeing her, and that keep my attention on her. I looked away for a moment and she was in front of me. Eric was near the crime scene.

It seems like everything stop, but us and she began to talk and said "TJ is not there anymore, he has gone on with the Lord", I just looked at her crying, slightly shaking my head. Then she said "Are you thirsty? Do you want something to drink? I get it for you." It was as if nothing was moving but her, she left and came back with the water to drink within seconds. She gave me a cup and filled it with water and said "take this cup and thirst no more" and it seems as quickly as she came, she was gone just as quick..

All I could think about was that she was my ministering angel. I thought to myself, she was sent by God to keep me focused and help me not to go crazy during this time of need. Later as my husband and I left the crime scene, he said "some lady in white gave me a drink of water and she left". All of a sudden "Jasmine starting to sing TJ is gone to Heaven over and over again, we all look at one another, because she was nowhere near the crime scene." It took us for a loop.

The thing that I remembered after leaving the crime scene was that I cried and cried, then after getting home, all I could think about was the memory of my son in the long black car with bullet holes in his body, one leg and one hand outside of the car door. That's all I could see for days, weeks and months and years, just about every day and night of my life, and though it's not as bad now, it's still there, just waiting for something to trigger it. Nevertheless, I am able to face it now and find healing, even though the triggers.

Let us continue our journey together – as you reflect...

As you reflect, it may be difficult, but it is intended to be therapeutic in nature with a destination of healing and liberation, so let us proceed with a portion of your story!

What do you remember with your loss?

Book Reader:

_____

_____

_____

_____

_____

_____

Let us continue my story –our journey...

What happened next?

We have arrived at the section of the book called "*I Remember*" – let's continue. I remember going to the morgue in Washington, DC, and though I was crying endlessly, I had to ID my son's body –..... my TJ was dead. This was one of the most difficult things I had to do, at this time. I had so much pain in my heart – pain that only one that was in my body could feel and understand. This was the type of pain that no one wants to or has to feel.

I can remember a lady coming out and explaining the step, before showing me a picture of my deceased son. The Autopsy Examiner said "*it would be too much to see the actual body for a mother*", and I simply cried and cried. As thoughts raced through my mind, I said to myself "Lord this must be a dream, please awaken me, this can't be, wake me up Lord" and I continued to cry. "Help me, please, I can't stand myself, it hurts", I cried to my husband, "it hurts,...... it hurts so bad". He said "I know Marion, I know", at that time no words could heal me. Sad situation when you feel that no one really can feel your pain, no one. Others can only image but in reality can't know.

As you continue to reflect, remember, it may be difficult, but the goal is therapeutic in nature with a destination of healing and liberation, so let us continue with another portion of your story!

What do you remember?

Book Reader:

_____

_____

_____

_____

_____

_____

_____

Chapter Two

Pre-Planning Activities And Thoughts

For days, I wasn't in a good condition to do anything. I remember family and friends coming by, and I tried remaining strong, for myself. It was so painful, my body was aching all over, and my head was throbbing, I felt like my head wanted to burst open and I was so tired and sleepy, but couldn't sleep nor eat. Nothing was working as I was always thinking of TJ,.... all the time! My mind continued racing with thoughts of my son being cold, freezing and needing heat as he lay in the morgue. You see, that's where my mind was at the time, due to the diminished state I was in during this season. I simply could not think clearly.

Let us continue my story –our journey ...

Have you ever had to make immediate plans for a loss love one?

Book Reader:

_____

_____

_____

_____

Chapter Three

Funeral Arrangements: When & How Were They Made?

Funeral Arrangements: When and how were they made?

I remember being at my home, not having gone to the funeral home as of yet and home was where I wanted to be. My family and I were around the table talking, and for some reason, I was being strong. I remember my husband, mother, mother-in-law (who I also call mom), and some other people around the table, but can't remember who the other people were. At that time, I really didn't care, not about the people, but just about the reasoning why we were at the table.

Pre-arrangements were made and once again, I was so tired. I remember crying and crying and then laying down on the bed. During this time my mother came in the room and lay beside me, putting her arms around me, looked at me and said "I know baby, I know" upon which time, I went to sleep for a little while. I was just so tired, and this was just making the pre-arrangements for the funeral, not at the final funeral home arrangements.

Nevertheless, when that final time arrived, I got sick,

felt lifeless and cried endlessly again the night and morning before making the final funeral arrangements. I remember feeling so sickly, I thought I was still dreaming, I told myself God will wake me up soon. God I know you are going to awaken me, this is only a dream. However, it wasn't a dream, it was real, it was happening and I had to move forward.

Let us continue my story – our journey …

Have you ever had to make immediate plans to bury your love one? What was that like?

Book Reader:

_____

_____

_____

_____

_____

_____

_____

_____

Chapter Four

The Impact Of Death Was So Painful

The impact of the death on me was so painful, I just wanted to die.

Physically – I didn't care how I looked, didn't comb my hair for what seemed like days. I didn't brush my teeth as I just didn't feel like it. Physically I wanted to die, ...it seem like I was already dead. In the flesh, I felt dead.

Mentally – I felt mentally crashed, sick inside out and couldn't stand to be alive, this was after reviewing the autopsy report, and I got very **Emotional** reading the immediate final cause of dead! My son, my TJ, as stated in the report (Certificate of Death) died due to gunshot wounds to the torso and upper extremity, perforating Lungs and Heart (he was shot nine [9] times).

I was so hurt, the pains felt like I was shot 9 times! Oh the pains, the pains, far beyond what many will ever know. Mentally, this was putting stress on my body, soul, and mind. This thing called **grief it's so painful**, I was going crazy inside. But when my good friends from NASA came over, I would act as if I was okay, maybe they knew the pain was too great, but when they would leave, I would cry and cry, O'Lord I cried, what am I to do?

I experienced this emotional rollercoaster, but couldn't help myself. Off and on, I would read the report, trying to come to grips with everything, but wanting to believe this was still just a dream. My mind was continually racing with so many thoughts, over and over again.

What about you? Let us continue our journey—with your story ...

What impacted you physically and mentally?

Book Reader:

_____

_____

_____

_____

_____

_____

_____

_____

_____

_____

After the funeral and my subsequent visit(s) to church….

Going to Church after the funeral was painful for me, because I just didn't want to go. It was so much going on, due to the death of my son TJ being ruled a Homicide. I couldn't sit through a church service without crying through the entire service, especially if one of the songs played was one that my son liked.

I remember one song in particular, that happened to be the church's theme song – "Hezekiah Walker: I need you to Survive *Lyrics*" https://www.youtube.com/watch?v=uMcJL_UDAvw and another song called "Jesus", which I loved. I couldn't bear to hear them at first made me think of TJ and the other, made me sad at the time, because it was a song I heard at the funeral.

My son TJ called me mostly every day. Something many others may take for granted, but the loss of such calls tormented me. All I wanted to do was hug my son again, touch him on his forehead, give him a big kiss on the cheek, and talk with him. Sometime by the end of each day I was completely drained and tired, but I continued with life best I could. I continued to move forward.

Consider your return to church or a place dear to you, but difficult to visit after your loss.

Let us continue our journey – and your story ...

How did you feel about going to church or a place of comfort after your lost?

Book Reader:

_____

_____

_____

_____

_____

_____

_____

_____

_____

Were your church family members and/ or organization participants very supported?

Book Reader:

_____

_____

Chapter Five

How Did This Grieving Pain Impact Work?

At times, I could work and work sometimes I simply couldn't. My close friends from NASA like Patricia, Malores, Cynthia, Roni, Olivia (R.I.P.), Tracey, Doris, and Anetra always checked up on me and told me they love me so much. I had another boss at NASA name Val Burr, she was good to me and she would say "I don't know all you going through, but I care and take as much time as you need to and that was all I needed to hear."

Whenever I would go to work, I had one supervisor by the name of Mr. Poston, who was the best boss ever, though he eventually left for another job, he made this season in my life a little more bearable. On the contrary, I had another supervisor who understood nothing, and that made me mad! She stated "that I had two weeks off and that should have been enough"!

What is enough? How could she determine how much time was enough? My son TJ had been shot 9 times, something she will likely never understand, unless it happens to one of her loved ones (something I wouldn't wish on my worst enemy). Nevertheless, I pray the Lord helps people to be more understanding! I remember clearly hearing her say, "I give you two weeks off that should have been enough time". Unfortunately, all she seemed to care about was getting the work done.

Sadly, many people want you to get back to your normal self, but don't understand that it's not going to happen that easily. My life was and will be changed forever. I became a different person then and still am now. I was changed forever when my son died. He didn't just die, he was murdered. You just don't get back to normal in a couple of weeks, months, or not even years; this thing called "grief" is very slow and likewise is recovery. I describe it like being on the highway, driving slow without an accident, and appearing to be going nowhere.

If you are or were employed at the time of your loss, think back and let us continue our journey – with your story...

How did the loss of a love one impact your workplace?

Book Reader:

_____

_____

_____

_____

Did your employer understand what you were going through at all?

Book Reader:

_____

_____

_____

_____

_____

_____

_____

Chapter Six

My Years Of Grief 1St Thru 6Th

First year

My first year was so hard; I had to maintain my sanity and sound mind, so that the case could go forward. I knew if I cried all the time, I would not be able to make it. So, a lot of time I hide my pain and how I felt. I call this part of my road of grief "**The Aftermath**". When you lose your loved one, many people may think that is it. But you have the aftermath of the death, **"Homicide"** of my son TJ (in my case), which was a living nightmare.

As before, during this time, I was not able to sleep for hours at a time. Adding to this, having detectives knocking at my door after midnight giving me info about the case added to my stress and I wasn't able to confide in anyone. You see I wanted to unburden my heart, reveal information to my friends, but couldn't, because it would hinder the case.

This went on for over a year, just this part. My husband and I also talked with the State Attorney on the case and this was hard as we had to go over things time and time again. This process made me sick to my stomach. For a moment, imagine not being able to eat, sleep or work at times. This was my life and this pattern was not good for me, or my husband.

This was a violent crime committed against my son TJ. This was an unimaginable act that was covered on the channel 5 Fox News – which did a special report by Paul Wagner on the story. In addition, the Washington Post's Colbert I. King did report on the story for the first year.

Let us continue our journey – with your story …

What was your 1st year of grief like?

Book Reader:

_____

_____

_____

_____

_____

_____

_____

_____

_____

_____

My Second Year of Grief 2nd Thru 6th

Second Year

The 2nd year was even harder for me due to the trial. It was court time, and all the evidence was in after over a year of investigations (TJ die July 9, 2002 and court started August 2003), it was now time to move forward. Read what the Washington Post had to say about it below:

Report by Washington Post on 8/23/2003.

"Sending Fear Back to the Street"
By Colbert I. King

It was a bad sign. Assistant U.S. Attorney Thomas DiBiase was well into his closing argument in the government's case against accused murderer Jayvon Marshman, reportedly a member of the notorious 1-7 crew in the Adams Morgan section of Northwest Washington, when a juror signaled that he had to go to the bathroom. Superior Court Judge Erik Christian abruptly halted the proceedings, and the jurors filed out, leaving the prosecutor with his partially delivered summation hanging in the air. This is a bad sign, at least for the government.

For the first time in more than 40 jury trials, a courtroom observer said, DiBiase found himself cut off in the midst of a final summing up. The unexpected toilet break was not the only unusual event in the case of United States v. Jayvon Marshman. Somewhere between the beginning of the week-long trial and the jury's verdict in Courtroom 302 of the H. Carl Moultrie Building on Wednesday afternoon, the government's seemingly airtight case against Marshman sprang a leak.

Yes, there was ample evidence at trial that 22-year-old Thomas "T.J." Holly was fatally wounded in an alley behind Champlain Street at 2:30 p.m. on July 9, 2002. Fifteen shots were fired from a Tech-9 semiautomatic weapon, nine ended up in T.J.'s body. Yes, there was evidence that T.J. wasn't a street dude. And yes, too, his presence in the Adams Morgan neighborhood could be explained, since he resided with his grandmother, who has lived in that community for 50 years.

There was no murder weapon, DNA or fingerprints. But the prosecutor did put on the stand four eyewitnesses -- all of whom knew defendant Marshman. One identified him as the man with the T-shirt pulled up over his head that shot T.J. and ran down the alley with a gun in his hand in the company of another man; three others testified to hearing gunshots and next seeing Marshman with a gun running down the alley along with another man.

The motive, said DiBiase, stemmed from a verbal

altercation a month earlier between T.J. and Marshman. In all, 16 witnesses were produced to buttress the government's case against Marshman. His lawyer, Jonathan Rapping of the Public Defender Service, attacked inconsistencies in the testimony of the government's eyewitnesses. And Marshman's sister gave testimony that suggested her brother couldn't have been near the scene at the time of the murder.

Rapping also presented the jury with an alternative version of events: that the prosecution's eyewitnesses were mistaken and probably influenced by the power of suggestion -- for example, by street rumors that circulated immediately after the shooting indicating Marshman was the one who did it, and the sight of Marshman walking in the company of a police officer toward the police district station following the shooting. The jurors, hearing it all, evidently didn't think the government met its burden of proof. They let Marshman walk. Not guilty on all three counts.

"The jury's decision takes us right back to July 9 a year ago," said T.J.'s father, Eric Jones, in a telephone interview shortly after the verdict. "It feels like that day all over again."

Jones described T.J., a graduate of Eleanor Roosevelt High School in Greenbelt and middle linebacker on the school's football team, as a "fun guy who carried a smile all the time. . . . The jury's action was unbelievable," Jones said.

"*The government had eyewitnesses who knew [Marshman] and grew up with him. People know what they saw. He ran right past friends.*" Moreover, witnesses on the stand "*pointed right to him.*" Yet the jury found him not guilty, Jones said in disbelief.

T.J.'s mother, Marion Jones, was equally distraught when we spoke Thursday morning. She was especially annoyed by the Post story that suggested her son was a member of a rival Adams Morgan gang. "*T.J. was not part of a gang,*" she said. "*He had no drugs in his system, but was shot in cold blood*" in the neighborhood where he lived with his grandmother.

Mrs. Jones was especially concerned about the fate of the witnesses, including a 12-year-old boy and a 17-year-old girl, who "*put their lives on the line*" by testifying against a reputed neighborhood gang member. Pointing to the verdict, and the fact that witnesses are now living in fear, Mrs. Jones said, "*That's exactly why people don't want to testify.*" Should they live in fear?

Mrs. Jones said she has attended at least 15 status hearings involving Marshman, but has never seen his parents in court. But members of 1-7 crew were in Judge Christian's courtroom on Tuesday. They were sitting behind me. At one point, their voices were so loud that the judge had to admonish them to take their conversation outside *the courtroom. Another member, a tall young man wearing a Wizards jersey with a baseball cap pulled down over his dreads, had to be told by the judge to remove his cap. For some, including a female prosecution witness, they posed an intimidating presence. She told the judge as much. The 1-7 was there all right. Now they have their man back.*

At this point, a clarification of the Post story may be in order. Jayvon Marshman was not jailed on the murder charge, as the story may have suggested. He was already behind bars when he was charged with T.J.'s murder. Marshman had entered a guilty plea on May 30, 2002, to carrying a pistol -- namely a .38-caliber revolver with six live rounds in the chamber -- without a license. He was sentenced on July 26, 2002, to three years in jail, with all but one year suspended and two years' probation.

Ah, Mr. Marshman. He said he was carrying the gun for his own protection. Perhaps so, seeing as how he was shot in the thighs a few weeks before T.J.'s murder. Marshman was walking on Ontario Road when a teenager sitting in the passenger seat of a passing car yelled "lay your bitch ass down," pulled out a dark-colored gun, and began firing at Marshman.

Jayvon Marshman is also no stranger to the criminal justice system. His gun possession offense was his fourth adult arrest and second conviction, according to court papers. He even made the newspapers three years ago while in a rehabilitation center in the Lancaster, Pa., area. Marshman was arrested and put in Lancaster County Prison in lieu of $40,000 bail on charges of simple assault, making terroristic threats and disorderly conduct. Threatening to shoot, kill and break a chair over the head of a rehab center staff member -- as reported by the Sunday News (Lancaster) -- can win you charges like that.

States one evaluative summary of Marshman in 2002: "He presents as an immature individual with no insight into the seriousness of carrying a weapon in the community."

Time passes, even years, but take a moment to reflect.

Let us continue our journey – with your story ...

What was your 2nd year of grief like?

Book Reader:

_____

_____

_____

_____

_____

My Third Year of Grief 3rd Thru 6th

Third year

Gun 'n' Run—D.C.'s Game

The Washington Post - Washington, D.C.

Author:	Colbert I. King
Date:	Nov 8, 2003
Start Page:	A.27
Section:	EDITORIAL
Text Word Count:	1180

A few minutes later we encountered Farhat Cheema walking east on Columbia Road. He was not as lucky as the folks at Casa Lebrato. Cheema owns Cash Depot down the block. He told of how an armed man entered his business a few months ago and attempted to hold up the place. Ignoring the weapon, Cheema grabbed the man and held on until his cousin came from behind the counter to help. They were still holding the robber when the cops arrived 18 minutes later. During the struggle, the robber managed to get off two shots, but no one was hit. He's now in jail, but Cheema expects him to be back on the streets after a year. "We'll just have to prepare for him," Cheema said with a shrug.

Streets near 17th and Euclid are the playground of Jayvon Marshman, reportedly a 1-7 member. He also was accused of shooting and killing Thomas "T.J." Holly in an alley behind Champlain Street on July 9, 2002, with a TEC-9 semiautomatic pistol. Four eyewitnesses -- all of whom knew Marshman -- testified in court to hearing shots and seeing him running through the alley behind Champlain with a gun in his hand at the time Holly was murdered. During the August trial, the prosecution produced 16 witnesses to buttress the government's case against Marshman, already a convicted felon with multiple adult arrests.

An officer observed a man, who turned out to be your Jayvon Marshman, reach into the left side of his black jacket, pull out a large black and silver object, and pass it over to another man, Alvin Headspeth, who stashed the object beneath a baby seat located under the rear passenger seat of a nearby Ford Expedition. The object, recovered by police, was reportedly a loaded, black-and- silver Lorcin 9mm semiautomatic handgun with a round in the chamber. After passing the weapon, your man Marshman allegedly ran south on 13th Street NW. Carrying a pistol without a license, as you know, is a no-no in the District. A D.C. Superior Court judge issued a warrant for his arrest on Oct. 22.

NOTE: There is more to this story above.

Well, I was in my 3rd year of grief when I wrote this and I was just letting that article really sink into my thoughts. Having so much pain, I recall noting, I MUST go through it. I MUST!!

Reading the article made me very sick, I felt ill and just couldn't get over how the laws protect the guilty. Feeling all of this, another year would go by and I suffer the *homicide survivor experience* with different emotions as follows:

- Shock - Disbelief
- Helplessness – I'm tormenting myself – What could I have done?
- Guilt – Like it was my fault.
- Fear – Feeling anxious/restless and helpless.
- Numbness – Kept a lot inside – not feeling anything sometimes.
- Frustration – Angry with myself and God.
- Stress – Tension, anxiety and worry.
- Depression – I was very sad and I wanted to die.

- Chronic Pain – It was in my heart, having panic attacks, came frequency.
- Pain – Unbearable and hurt.
- Acceptance – This came later, but I prayed with God and He said "my daughter is at peace, rest and just be still and take day-by-day."

Some of these emotions were intense and I often had some suppressed feeling resurface years later after the homicide. Nonetheless, this is grief/grieving and they are an individual process that differs for everyone. It took me some time to begin to heal and recover because losing a loved one is not easy and trying to process it is extremely difficult to say the least.

My 3rd year was if it was the 2nd year, because of the jury finding him not guilty. I cried so much for months. In addition, I started having anxiety pains that felt like a heart attacks. The doctor told me that I could die of a broken heart, if I didn't take care of myself. Therefore, I started going to a support group called **"Maryland Crime Victims' Resource Center, Inc. (MCVRC), Family Forever Support Group** and **The Compassionate Friends (TCF)" meetings.** This was part of my journey for healing and recovery.

If it's been more at least three years, what has it been like?

Let us continue our journey – with your story ...

What was your 3rd year of grief like?

Book Reader:

_____

_____

_____

_____

_____

_____

_____

_____

What types of emotions did you experience?

Book Reader:

_____

_____

_____

_____

_____

_____

_____

_____

My Four Year of Grief 4th Thru 6th

By year four, I was recovering, though slowly from my loss. I really started to take care of myself, because I had my other family members, who cared about me and wanted me to get better. I end up going to more support groups and ended up facilitating support groups for TCF. I wanted to help other people in their grief process. I believe that talking with the doctor awakened me when he said I could die of a broken heart with these panic attacks. Those were some of the things I began to do. Consider the following:

The Washington Times

www.washingtontimes.com

_____

Tearful service remembers victims of violence

By Arlo Wagner

THE WASHINGTON TIMES

Published April 11, 2005

Marion M. Jones blinked back tears repeatedly yesterday as she made the keynote address at a memorial service for 561 Southern Maryland crime victims.

"This is probably the hardest thing I have ever had to do," said Mrs. Jones, 48, of Clinton, as she described how she learned that her son, Thomas B. Holly, III, known as TJ, 22, was fatally shot nine times in 2002 in the District.

A crowd of about 600 listened silently and nodded their heads in agreement in the auditorium of the Student Center of Prince George's County Community College in Largo.

It was the 16th annual statewide Memorial Service for Crime Victims and Their Families. Similar programs were conducted by state's attorney's offices in Dorchester, Harford and Washington counties.

"It's important for survivors to be treated with respect and dignity, to receive compassionate treatment," said Prince George's State's Attorney Glenn F. Ivey.

Later, commemorative certificates were presented to Mr. Ivey and to Roberta Roper, who established the

Stephanie Roper Committee and Foundation 23 years ago, after her daughter was kidnapped, assaulted, raped and killed in Prince George's County.

The Stephanie Roper Committee has been incorporated with the Maryland Crime Victims' Resource Center, and Mrs. Roper is chairwoman of the board of directors.

Two slain sons were the incentive for Paula Davis, 48, of Olney, to attend the service in Prince George's. Daryl V. Lash Jr., 22, was stabbed twice in the District on Aug. 20, 2002.

His older brother, Rashad I. Matthews, 24, was shot when he went to a Rockville motel to pick up a friend on March 20, 2004.

A $10,000 reward will be paid to a person who provides information leading to the capture of either killer, said Mrs. Davis, who was wearing a black T-shirt emblazoned with photos of her sons and the words, "You're complete and smiling now that you're with your baby brother."

During the program, an emotional Mrs. Davis had to leave the hall, followed by Mr. Lash's girlfriend, Shannon Cubbage, 22, of Hyattsville, who went to comfort her grief-stricken friend.

Trevon Crosby, 10, sang "The Star-Spangled Banner," and about two dozen children followed a bagpiper, carrying a net bedecked with white stars that they draped under a sign that read, "Their Light Still Shines."

Mrs. Jones expressed bitterness -- "I was angry with God" -- after the man suspected of being her son's killer was acquitted.

But, she said, her religious faith became a source of comfort. She urged the audience to express hope to gain comfort.

"Hope means to open people's ears," Mrs. Jones said. "If we move forward in our loved one's memory, we will give hope to others."

As I proceed toward my 5th year you will see other things I have accomplish to help me move forward in my grief.

Let us continue our journey – with your story ...

Have you ever spoke out about your loss love one to a group, public or private? Or maybe even an individual. If so, reflect and journal.

Book Reader:

_____

_____

_____
_____

What was it like to speak out?

Book Reader:

_____
_____
_____
_____
_____
_____
_____
_____

Do people say things you didn't like? Yes or No

Book Reader:

_____
_____
_____
_____
_____
_____
_____

How did it make you feel?

Book Reader:

_____

_____

_____

_____

_____

_____

_____

_____

My Five Year of Grief 5ᵗʰ Thru 6ᵗʰ

Sure, I had made it five years after such a difficult loss of my son TJ. But the 5ᵗʰ year was still hard, and the only way I could move forward was to keep my focus on God. I knew that this was the place He wanted me to be, in order to help others to move forward, as He helped me. I was blessed to speak on multiple occasions to grieving friends and family members from various walks of life, all in efforts to facilitate healing and recovery from the loss of a loved one (s)!

KEYNOTE SPEAKER RESUME

April 10, 2005, Guest Speaker:

Spoke at a memorial service in the auditorium for 600
Southern Maryland crime victims.

Location:
Student Center of Prince George's
County Community College, Largo, MD

December 11, 2005, Guest Speaker:

Spoke at The Compassionate Friends,
District of Columbia
Chapter for "World Wide Candle Lighting Service"

Location:
Howard University's Blackburn Center
The Reading Room
2400 Sixth Street, NW
Washington, DC

January 31, 2006, Guest Speaker:

Reading a poem (Moving Forward) at the Stepping Up
Program in Prince George's County.

Location: Riverdale Baptist

March 11, 2006, Guest Speaker:
Spoke at National Sigma Week, the ladies of
Zeta Tau Sigma

Alumnae Chapter of Sigma Gamma Rho Sorority, Inc.,
annual Sigma Youth Symposium.
Location: University of Maryland College
College Park, MD

In my 4th and 5th year, I had notice that among the
African Americans, it seemed as though I was still searching
to find others like me. Others that may have a story to tell.
Unfortunately, I could hardly find any story that spoke of
what I and many others in the African American culture was
facing. I wanted to know how other went through coping
with the loss of a child. I found that it was very difficult,
because no one was telling their stories.

I still find myself going through these days without
anyone telling their stories (on a greater scale), except
maybe in a support group or television through the media.
I wanted to hear stories of real life experiences, so I can

really relate my feeling with others in an effort to help my process of healing and recovery.

I talked with Dr. Ruff about this on several occasions and she shared the same feeling as I. I was so pleased when she decided to spearhead a project to fill this void. She formally invited me to join her in writing the story of our group of African Americans consisting of bereaved parents and siblings that had experienced the loss of a loved one. Unfortunately, it didn't happen because they didn't want to participate; some said "it was too painful", and I get it, but we MUST help others by telling our story.

However, it got to the point where I had to do it alone, and the results are what you now read. I'm so excited about writing my own individual story because, I have been working on it for awhile. I am equally excited that you've joined me on this journey and began to share your own story. Sure, it's not an easy thing to do, but we MUST share, so we can move forward in our grief and help others to do the same.

Let us continue our journey – with your story ...

What do you remember about the 5th year of grief (if it's been that long) or any continued grief?

Book Reader:

_____

_____

_____

_____

_____

_____

_____

So, if you are at your 5th year of grief, or continue to grieve, how do you now feel?

Book Reader:

_____

_____

_____

_____

_____

_____

_____

Help for you – on our journey...

I would say if you are at your 5th year of grief (or it's been an extending period) and haven't received any help, or joined a support group; or still crying at night and maybe when you take a shower; or you get in your car, drive and cry, then it is time not only to consider, but get involved. You do not have to go through grief alone. Others that have experienced similar (but different) loses, can assist you on this journey to healing and recovery.

If years after the loss, you cannot bear the mention and/or remark of your loved ones name; if you find yourself sleeping throughout the day; if you don't participate with family and friends in your normal everyday activities; or you do things to "numb yourself" to escape your grief, those are your warning signs, that you are not coping well. Please seek the assistance or counseling you need to begin healing. This is one of my prayers for you.

Grief is a life-long, emotional journey that is sometimes like a roller coaster, but it's doesn't mean you can't lead a happy life or work toward it, the choice is yours. No doubt that missing a special day or milestone like a birthday or the anniversary of their death will likely continue to sadden you to a certain extent. Even thinking of your loved one missing a special day or milestone in your life, may make you sad and cry, but don't worry yourself about it to a point of not being able to cope, you are not alone!

Allow yourself the opportunities to talk about the

circumstances of your loss, your feelings of loss and loneliness. And sure, continue to allow yourself time to grieve, as grieving is a life long journey. Walk slowly in it and even if you fall, get up slowly. Keep going through so you can cope in a positive way and stay healthy in your grief, by continually moving forward.

Note, there is no expiration date on grief. Again, remember it's a life long journey. Grief never fully goes away; we just learn to cope better. This doesn't mean however, you can't live a happy and productive life. What it does mean is that your loved one will be with you always, no matter what, because there is no expiration date, ever.

Also, keep in mind, as grief never goes away, there is no right or wrong way to do the work of grief. Take it one moment, minutes, days or weeks, months, or years at a time. Grief will take on different forms in different people. In addition, the different circumstances under which your love one(s) died can influence your feelings of grief. Always remember people cope with the loss of a loved one in different ways. Again, when you are going through your grieving, please seek counseling or join a support group. Try to enjoy a good family member or friend seeking to listen to your story and be a part of your journey to healing and recovery.

Let us continue our journey – with your story …

How did you deal with your grief?

Book Reader:

_____

_____

_____

_____

_____

_____

_____

_____

_____

_____

_____

_____

_____

_____

_____

_____

_____

Consider the following links that are great in assisting you through this process:

http://www.helpguide.org/articles/grief-loss/coping-with-grief-and-loss.htm

http://www.psychologistanywhereanytime.com/emotional_problems_psychologist/psychologist_grief.htm

http://www.cancer.org/acs/groups/cid/documents/webcontent/002826-pdf.pdf

https://www.compassionatefriends.org/Brochures/understanding_grief_when_your_child_dies.aspx

http://www.terynobrien.com/2013/11/21/15-things-i-wish-id-known-about-grief/

My Six Year of Grief 6th Thru 6th

As my 6th year of grief was approaching I couldn't believe it. I was now even more motivated to write a small booklet of my poems and others inspirational poems given to me in the process of my grief. I wanted to show as many people that may be grieving how I was now able to process my grief and provide my writings to assist on their journey. All in an effort to help them open up and get through their grief more, and move a little further along to live life.

Over the years I have compiled small inspirational booklets of short stories of some of the amazing things that happened each year at my son's grave site on both his birthdays and anniversary dates of his death. Nevertheless, it has been several years and I'm still on my journey of grief and I pray that something said in this book or a reflection from you may inspire and help you, just as God has helped me.

Approaching the anniversary of my son TJ's death, 7/9/2008, (which was leading to the 6th year), another tragedy struck (June, 19, 2008) as my oldest son James was killed in an auto accident.

Now, a new loss and the beginning of a new story, again. Pain, is how I'm feeling at this time, pain all over again. I pray, "God give me the strength, here goes another journey soon to begin again." **Now ask yourself these questions:**

- When will we ever be able to thoroughly and truly explain the pain that overtakes your soul as parents when you lose a child or a love one?

Similar to my Epigraph, if we asked....

What do you call a Child that loses a parent?
The answer would be *an orphan*.

If we said a Man that loses his wife?
The answer would be *a widower*.

And if we said a Woman who loses her husband?
The answer would be *a widow*.

So we ask each other what is the name for a parent(s) that loses a child? And we realize there is no answer; because there is *no word to describe the pain*.

Could such a loss be called Pain, because it's So Great for there is no word to describe loss but Pain?

Let us continue our journey – and navigate through the pain, with your story ...

What do you remember about the 6th year of grief (or your extended period of grief)?

Book Reader:

_____

_____

_____

_____

_____

_____

_____

_____

Have you moved forward in your grief yet? Yes or No

Book Reader:

_____

_____

_____

_____

_____

Chapter Seven

How Are You Feeling Now?

After such loss with TJ and now the loss of my second son, my heart is in more pain. My oldest son James, is now gone and the pain hurts more, seemingly starting all over again. My need was and now and still is prayers, so please keep me lifted. I know that God got me through the first, and he will get me through this one (James Douglas R.I.P.).

Some may ask, how I got through some of my grief journey or how I got over my grief. But I must remind some and tell all, grief isn't just something to get over, it will be with you forever, likely until death. However, with God, I have accepted my purpose, plan, and path (3P's) in life and it's my story and I'm sticking to it. God is the only one who can truly and thoroughly get you through the heart aches and pains of such lose and do it as no one else can. For those that have experience such deliverance, won't He do it? My answer is "Yes he will…!"

Feel free to tell me – how you feel, and what's on your mind so far from reading my story of "A Grieving Mother". Please email me at: mmjonesagrievingmother@gmail.com

Let us continue our journey – with your story …

What do you remember doing in your 7th year of grief (or whatever point you may be at now)?

Book Reader:

_____

_____

_____

_____

_____

_____

_____

_____

_____

_____

_____

_____

Chapter Eight

What Has Been Most Helpful Along Your Grief Journey?

My grief goes on, because I've had another loss of my oldest son James, killed in an auto accident. What do I do? I asked God why? And again, I searched for a reason and I heard the Lord say "Marion you have given them as a living sacrifice to help save your family", and I got angry and mad. I said to the Lord as I cried and cried, "my family doesn't appreciate anything, why, why? And as He softly whispered in my ear, "get up Marion and move forward, walk in it, remember the cause". I was in pain for days and weeks; I began to praise God and worship Him again and told Him, I loved Him. I kept on singing and singing, this went on for months.

Now, you probably ask how much more can this lady take? Well guest what? Eight months later my daughter TaSha was diagnosed with 4 stage breast cancer! I didn't even have time to grieve my oldest son James' death. I remembered my daughter telling me about her cancer diagnosis and I recall how hurt she was having to tell me after having just lost her older brother James. What a tragedy for both of us and how do I get through it as well as her?

As I'm suffering extreme sorrow and pain at this point, it simply hurts. The question again for the 3rd time – Why God? God, why did this happen again? It hurt so bad, so bad! I cried and cried again and again, it seemed like the crying went on forever. When was it ever going to end, the hurt, the pain and the sorrow in my life? How does a grieving mother cope with this situation? I held on and God continued to show me how. To God be the Glory!

Let us continue our journey – with your story …

If you are still hurting and have wondered when the pain would subside. When and if it was ever going to end, the hurt, the pain and the sorrow in my life? Please share your thoughts!

Book Reader:

_____

_____

_____

_____

_____

_____

How does a grieving mother cope with this situation?

Book Reader:

_____

_____

_____

_____

_____

_____

_____

_____

Added Grief….

Now, with more chapters of grief in my life, my sons (TJ & James) gone, and now TaSha was diagnosis with 4 Stage Breast Cancer, I still had to maintain life and move forward. The story of my life goes on and I continued moving forward in it. Although I didn't like what had taken place, I knew that I would surely die if I didn't stay focused on God! For me, He was and is the only way through it all!

I pray for the living, which was my daughter, asking God to let her live and not die. Does anyone remember the story in the Bible where the man was given more years on his life? I have to pray and pray, day in and day out, night in and night out. This is the scripture I prayed and asked of God – for more years with my daughter, see below:

Isaiah 38:5 (King James Version) – **recommend you reading the whole chapter Isaiah 38**

> **5** Go, and say to Hezekiah, Thus saith the LORD, the God of David thy father, I have heard thy prayer, and I have seen thy tears: behold, I will add unto thy days fifteen years.

I am extremely grateful that my daughter TaSha overcame this cancer by the grace of God and I still have her. For that, I continue to Give God The Glory! Through it all, nonetheless, I still have my days, but I'm moving forward through a grieving mother's journey, and it hurts. But I have work to be done saith the Lord! People may not understand, but it's not for them to understand, he says "my sheep hear my voice", these are word of scripture that are close to my heart.

John 10:26 – 30

> [26]But ye believe not, because ye are not of my sheep, as I said unto you.

> [27]My sheep hear my voice, and I know them, and they follow me:

^{28}And I give unto them eternal life; and they shall never perish; neither shall any man pluck them out of my hand.

^{29}My Father, which gave them me, is greater than all; and no man is able to pluck them out of my Father's hand.

^{30}I and my Father are one.

Let us continue our journey – with your story …

What is your relationship with God (if any)?

Book Reader:

_____

_____

_____

_____

_____

_____

_____

Who inspired you to get better?

Book Reader:

_____

_____

_____

_____

_____

_____

_____

What Bible scriptures (if any) or words of encouragement helps you get through your grief journey.

Book Reader:

_____

_____

_____

_____

_____

_____

_____

_____

Chapter Nine

Who Has Been Helpful To You?

As previously mentioned, some of my family and friends from NASA Goddard has helped me through difficult times as I was going the road sand valleys of grief. More importantly, for me, my God has kept and keeps me going. I remember saying "God grant me the serenity to accept the things I can't change, the courage to change the things I can, and the wisdom to know the difference". We always say this at the end of one of the support group meeting.

The most helpful thing going through my grief has been my faith and belief in God. I want to always talk to God! And I am thankful He continues to help me as He provides answers and guidance to my questions. I knew and learn that I can be upset with God and he will not get angry at me, but speak to me in a sweet voice. God spoke with me directly, and has given and continues to give me answers and directions at all times.

I've learned to mediate and communicate, so I can always have a personal experience with God. He is my source of strength and gives me comforter when I'm sad. He always places a song in my heart.

Let us continue our journey – with your story …

What song or songs help you get through your grief journey?

Book Reader:

_____

_____

_____

_____

_____

_____

Who has been helpful to you -- still today on your grief journey?

Book Reader:

_____

_____

_____

_____

_____

Chapter Ten

Impact Of The Death On Other Family Members

Subtitles:
* The organizations that were helpful to me.
* What has been least helpful?

Impact of the death on other family members

Many family members cannot find ways to deal with the loses from their past and as of the present time, still find them difficult and it effects them daily. They are so hurt and the pain is great for them as well. Some of them are not able to cope as I am now. For example, I notice how my mother displays her hurt, having lost both of her grandsons and it is clear that she misses them both as she talks about them all the time, which in itself can be good and therapeutic.

It is my prayer, however, that it would not be just strangers, but also family and friends will read this book and be blessed by its contents. Nevertheless, even beyond this book, there are helpful resources and organizations available that were instrumental in my journey towards healing and recovery as well.

The organizations that were helpful to me were:

1. **The Compassionate Friends**

http://www.compassionatefriends.org/home.aspx

2. **I facilitated at this chapter for 3 ½ years:**

The Compassionate Friends of Prince George's County - Former Co-Chapter Leader

> **UNITED PARISH OF BOWIE**
> **Second Thursdays at 7:00 pm**
> **Jan Withers 301-627-7315**

3. **Family & Friends Forever Support Group**
   Jan Withers 301-627-7315

4. **MADD**

   Jan Withers, National President, Mothers Against Drunk Driving (MADD)

   http://www.whitehouse.gov/champions/ drug-control/jan-withers

   New National President Jan Withers Begins Term MADD Maryland is honored to announce: As of July 1st, MADD has a new National President— Maryland's own Jan Withers. Jan joined MADD in 1992, after her 15-year-old daughter, Alisa Joy,

was killed by an underage drinker who chose to drive after consuming numerous beers. She first volunteered by sharing her story and lobbying for tougher legislation. However, over the years, she became even more active in her home state of Maryland and eventually became a member of the MADD National Board of Directors.

5. **Maryland Crime Victims' Resource Center, Inc. (MCVRC)**
   http://www.mdcrimevictims.org/
   1001 Prince Georges Blvd # 750, Upper Marlboro - (301) 952-0063

6. **Anne Arundel County Chapter of The Bereaved Parents of the USA**
   http://www.aacounty-md-bereavedparents.org/

7. **Parents Of Murdered Children (POMC)**
   http://www.pomc.com/

What has been least helpful?

A negative person that is not educated on grief has no clue as to what I'm going through on my road of grief. I don't like it when they complain, but I'm even learning to deal with the negative stuff they bring to life. I simply say "Whatever problems, situations, issues and circumstances that they are going through are mediocre to me." I have learned to focus on the big picture and not get caught up on how they attempt to frame life!

Consider the following link for additional assistance:
http://griefminister.com/2015/07/29/do-not-fall-for-these-11-myths-about-grief/

Who & what has been the least helpful going through your grief?

Book Reader:

_____

_____

_____

_____

_____

_____

_____

Chapter Eleven

What Has Pushed Your Buttons (Irked You To No End?)

How did you cope with it?

I have come to realize that all people are not as compassionate as I may be and are not as concerned about really knowing about the hows and whys connected to what we are going through. Some of the questions and statements such people tend to ask and say are as follows:

- How many children do you still have?

- Well, at least you have other children.

- Are you still going to that support group meeting?

Even within the support group, people don't always think clearly and say things such as follows:

This is one thing that irked me to no end, when people at support group say "at least you have more children, that was my only child. I love my group, but hear me out, *just because I have more children and you have none, doesn't mean it hurts any less!* I still have to get to the place of healing and recovery from just that loss of one, even if we have more children! It doesn't matter one left or more children left, we all grieve.

It must hurt tremendously if you have only one child

that dies, and we can't take your grief away from you, so we must be considerate of all that have lost any and not take their grief away, for all hurt. This is just an educational lesson that I have learned in group.

Don't forget, all that are in groups such as the one I was with have had a loss – and that's the most important thing to consider. Again, such a loss, pains us all. Nevertheless, I don't get upset when someone says that anymore, because I know they are going through some things. It has been an educational experience for me also.

Body (ex. Exercise) - This didn't happen overnight, but took about three (3) years for me before I even thought about me personally. I've learned to exercise my body through praying, reading the Bible (Word of God) and eating right. Thankfully, my friend Patricia was helping me as well to think on good things.

Mind (ex. Journaling or counseling) I have been able to journal, be creative in my jewelry making, read spiritual books, and once again read and study scriptures, which has helped me tremendously. Also, receiving counseling has been good for me. Not from just anyone however, but from someone who has experience such loss and has been on the road to healing and recovery. One counselor told me "she lost her dog" can you believe that, my child was not a dog or how can you compare a child to a dog. End of story.

Spirit (ex. Prayer or more church going). Prayer and church becomes an obvious many people will direct you to. However, as I mentioned, such things, particularly the latter was difficult for me in the beginning stages of grief. I was so mad at God, but my good friend and Jan Withers' my co-leader of TCF told me "God could handle it all by himself". In other words God was big enough to handle my anger, yet love me enough to get me through it.

Let us continue our journey – with your story…

What things irk you as you were going through your grief?

Book Reader:

_____

_____

_____

_____

_____

_____

_____

_____

Chapter Twelve

Things That Was Helpful Going Through My Grief

Subtitle:
What else have you done in the following areas?

What else have you done in the following areas?

I have been involved in church, writing poems, and guest speaking (at three different colleges -- P.G. College, Howard University, & Maryland University College) helped me. Also, "Stepping-Up Program" – People in Prince George's taking action against crime. Currently, my growth is with Fox Talkz Toastmasters, were I'm learning to become a speaker.

Spirituality: Religion, prayer etc.

Church – being active in things to help you heal. I liked listening to Pastor Derek Gier of Grace Church, Dumfries, VA – FM 105.1 every morning at 5:00a.m., he has helped me for many, many years.

Outreach—helping other

Former Co-Chapter Leader of TCF of Prince George's County for 3 ½ years. I liked meeting with the group every 2nd Thursday of each month. In addition doing a TCF Newsletter for the chapter was exciting and rewarding. Further, I would receive calls anytime and I enjoyed helping other through, just like other got me through. I thank God for the help of others, especially TCF members and my friend Jan.

A— a new Attitude—if so what is it?

I made a promise to myself to always help someone going through loss as I continually remember my sons TJ and James. In doing so, I'm forever reminded that he didn't die in vain. This new attitude about life keeps me "Moving Forward" towards my goal of taking care of myself. This new attitude is life long and a forever process that will get me through my grief.

Reinvestment: What you did and are doing in any of the following areas?

Advocacy—helping others

Policy--Getting laws changed

Although I am doing many things, the latter is something I need to work on. Nonetheless, as I'm processing other things – new people are coming to the support group and many are getting help based on their situations or circumstances.

Education (giving talks to others) about gun safety, grief, and grieving etc.

Memorials—continuing bonds. How have you remembered your child/sibling over the years?

What things helped you as you were going through your grief?

Book Reader:

_____

_____

_____

_____

_____

_____

_____

_____

_____

_____

Chapter Thirteen

My Messages And Suggestions To The Bereaved & Newly Bereaved.

Subtitles:
* What lesson have you learned?
* What do you wish you had done differently?

Messages, suggestions, and / or possibilities for the newly bereaved:

1. You cry when you less expect it.
2. Things that you use to like, you don't anymore
3. Things seem meaningless.
4. You may not have the same friends.
5. You may not want to work anymore.
6. I believe that you can't go through your grief alone; you have to invite God in to help you go through your grief.

What lessons have you learned?

You have to write your feelings throughout your

own grief journey. People can give you advice and encouragement, but only God can help to heal your heart.

What do you wish you had done differently?

Quit my job and moved away, I know that for me it would have help me, but to each their own.

Please list any other parting thoughts or comments.

On my grief journey, finding emotional healing has come through writing, photography, and finding other creative ways to express my feelings, including that of making jewelry. Sometimes I don't see myself as very creative, but it gives me peace of mind. During my grief journey, I discovered healing to becoming whole. I know God loves me and He will keep me moving forward.

Feel free to share my story with those you encounter and please encourage them to stay focus on God as he will direct your path. In my house on my refrigerator I have a word that I live by that says "God uses our difficulties to develop our characters", please remember this and remain focused.

What has helped you after reading this book?

Book Reader:

_____

_____

_____

_____

_____

_____

_____

_____

Let me know what other things were able to help you that I didn't experience?

Book Reader:

_____

_____

_____

_____

_____

_____

_____

_____

_____

_____

What thing irks you as you were going through your grief?

Book Reader:

_____

_____

_____

_____

_____

_____

_____

Would you recommend this book to other? Yes or No

If yes or no please explain (optional)...

Book Reader:

_____

_____

_____

_____

_____

_____

_____

Thank you for your input.

Helpful Scriptures

* Time.............................. Ecclesiastes 3:1-8

* Patience.......................... Romans 15:4-5

* Love .... 1 John 4:7

* Hope.............................. Job 14:7

* Faith.............................. Mark 11:22

* Care .... 1 Peter 5:7

* Heal.............................. Ecclesiastes 3:3

* Forgive.......................... Matthew 6:15

* Peace............................ Psalms 34:14

**********Sharing Your Story is Caring***********

Your Words May Lead To Another's Deliverance!

The End Comments

Morning is a constant reminder that things will never be the same. So, what do we need during a time of grief? -- Scriptures, a song, encouragement, family, friends, and even sharing our story. And, without a doubt—God! May He Bless You Greatly As You Continue Your Journey!

Moving forward, know that anything could trigger an uncontrollable emotion from a lost; you could still hear a song on the radio, a commercial on TV, seeing a mom shopping with her child. This will sometimes catch you in the wind, but know that if you stand strong in your faith, God will take you through it all the way.

I began my journey with a grieving heart, and when your grief is new it's overwhelmingly, very painful and scary. Death makes people uncomfortable, so they fear it and they have unrealistic expectations as to how you should feel when you grieve. Remember there is no timeframe on how long you grieve, just grieve. Many are very uncomfortable with your grief and may want it to go away as soon as possible. They attempt to relax you, encourage you, and try to make you comfortable and give you advice to "get over it and get on with your life.

I pray that my journey as a grieving mother has helped

put hope back into your life so that you can have healing in your heart.

Finally, I hope my effort to help those families who have lost a child be able to feel a sense of moving forward in their journey and will be encouraged and able to share a personal story of grief and healing along the way.

THE END

Contact:

Email <u>mmjonesagrievingmother@gmail.com</u> if you have any questions, concerns or comments after reading this book. May God Bless You and Your Family!

About The Author

Marion M Jones has been "A Grieving Mother" since 2002, losing two (2) sons she decided to express her pain by writing and becoming book author. She has climbed to the top to survive, and move forward in her grief. She and her husband share their home current now in Southern California with other family members.

Marion work with parents who have lost a loved one and are tired of feeling overwhelmed with sadness and hurt. She help them regain joy, peace, and love in their lives.

Marion is also best known for supporting other grieving parents. Visit her at www.agrievingmother.com.

Printed in the United States
By Bookmasters